rice
cooker

rice
cooker

Brigid Treloar

APPLE

Contents

Introducing the rice cooker

Why use a rice cooker?

- Rice cookers are simple and convenient to use, and are also inexpensive.
- Amazingly versatile and durable, rice cookers not only cook food but keep it warm and effectively reheat leftovers.
- They are safe to turn on and set to cook without the risk of burning food.
- Foods cooked in a rice cooker retain their nutrients.
- Cooking in a rice cooker is almost as fast as using a microwave, but, unlike the microwave, the rice cooker does not cook unevenly and therefore does not create cold spots in the food.

What can be cooked in a rice cooker?

Almost anything. You may be surprised at how many foods in addition to rice and whole grains can be cooked in a rice cooker, from soups, stews and pasta to vegetables, eggs and desserts.

How does a rice cooker work?

There are different types of rice cookers, but the most popular is the electric rice cooker. Often made of stainless steel, it consists of a rice cooker chamber with a spring loaded heating element at the bottom. A removable metal bowl, often nonstick and sometimes fitted with handles, sits in the rice cooker on the heating plate. Bowls with a nonstick surface are best, but if the surface is not nonstick, spray it with vegetable oil cooking spray before using. A lid seals the rice cooker. Some models have a metal or glass lid, others a vacuum-sealed lid and still others a locking lid that seals the cooker and keeps rice moist (see picture page 8). The amount of liquid used in an electric rice cooker, including for rice, is usually less than the amount used in a pot on the stove top, as the lid seals the cooker, resulting in less evaporation.

Most electric rice cookers have "cook" and "warm" buttons. The cooker is designed to boil water fast when the "cook" button is pushed, then automatically reduce the heat as the heating element senses the water is absorbed and rice is cooked. The cooker switches to "warm" and can hold food safely at 140°F (60°C) without burning it, from five to twelve hours, depending on the manufacturer.

The capacity of rice cookers is measured by the "rice cup," which is smaller than a conventional measuring cup. Usually, domestic models hold a range of 2 to 10 rice cups of uncooked rice. Rice cookers are sold with a rice cup. The inside of the rice cooker bowl is marked with measurements that correlate with the capacity of the rice cup. The proportion of water to rice is important, so be sure to use the same measuring cup for both rice and water.

Types of rice cookers

On/off rice cookers

- Usually the least expensive type, this electric on/off unit cooks rice, then turns off automatically. It does not have a light that indicates when the rice is cooked. The rice cooker bowl is usually not nonstick, and steamer racks are often not included.
- Cook and keep warm. Once the rice has cooked, the electric cooker reduces the heat automatically and keeps the rice warm for a period of time that varies from machine to machine, usually 5 to 12 hours. Nonstick pans and one, and sometimes two, steamer trays or racks may be included.

Fuzzy logic rice cookers

- Basic. The term "fuzzy logic" refers to microchip technology that makes a cooker more sophisticated, albeit more expensive. An electronic menu offers specific settings for different rice varieties. Some models include a slow-cook cycle for soups and stews, a reheat function that warms rice in 5–10 minutes and maintains the heat, a quick-cook function that bypasses the rice soak time, a setting for choosing the preferred rice texture, from soft to firm, and a timer for presetting cooking times up to 24 hours ahead (see picture below, center).

On/off electric rice cooker with metal non-locking lid

Microchip "fuzzy logic" rice cooker with vacuum-sealed locked lid

Vacuum-sealed electric rice cooker

Rice pot

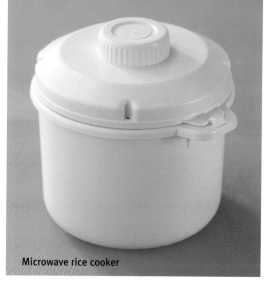

Microwave rice cooker

- Induction heating. This state-of-the-art, yet more expensive rice cooker can determine cooking times for different types of rice and food and can even compensate for measuring errors to produce perfectly cooked rice. A powerful magnetic field is created, so cooking starts immediately, even in the center of the food, resulting in fast, even cooking.

Rice pot

This large, metal stove-top pot often has a nonstick surface for easy cleaning. It should have a tight-fitting metal or glass lid, and some come with steamer basket inserts. Buy good quality, or the heat tends to be uneven. There

are also clay rice cookers (see picture above left). As neither has the automatic cook and keep warm functions of the electric rice cookers, you need to monitor the cooking time.

Microwave rice cooker

An inexpensive option, this cooker consists of a plastic bowl that is safe to use in a microwave as well as clean in a dishwasher. The bowl has a tight-fitting lid. This type is not usually intended for cooking large quantities. To use this cooker, cook on high for 5 minutes, then reduce to medium for 12–15 minutes for white rice and 35–45 minutes for brown. Then stand 5 minutes, covered.

Accessories

Some are included with the cookers; others are optional.

RICE CUP This plastic cup, supplied with the rice cooker holds 4½–5 ounces (140–150 g) of uncooked rice and 5½ fluid ounces (165 ml) of water if filled to the water level marked on the cup or 6 fluid ounces (180 ml) if filled to the brim. The inside of the rice cooker bowl has marks that correlate to the capacity of the rice cup. If you misplace the cup, use a standard measuring cup (1 cup/8 fl oz/250 ml) for both the rice and the water, following the cooking guide on page 17. When you use a standard cup, recipes may need to be adjusted accordingly. The recipes in this book use a standard measuring cup for rice and liquid, not a rice cup.

STEAMER TRAYS Some rice cookers are designed to accommodate one or two trays, racks or baskets for steaming foods, especially vegetables. As these foods steam in the tray, rice, pasta or more vegetables can be cooked underneath it.

RETRACTABLE OR REMOVABLE CORD The power cord on some models retracts into the appliance and the cord on others can be removed. This feature is an advantage when storing the cooker and when bringing it from the kitchen to the table for serving.

CARRY HANDLE A handle is useful for taking the cooker to the table for serving.

RICE PADDLE/SPATULA This plastic or wooden paddle or spatula is for fluffing cooked rice and for serving it. Metal utensils should not be used as they can scratch the nonstick surface of the rice cooker bowl. Some models have a spatula holder that attaches to the side of the cooker.

PLASTIC TONGS Tongs made of plastic or coated in plastic are preferred over metal as they do not scratch the nonstick surface of the rice cooker bowl.

COLANDER/STRAINER A colander or strainer is useful for draining rice. It should have fine mesh so the grains do not fall through the grid.

Care and cleaning

- A nonstick surface on the rice cooker bowl ensures easy cleaning.
- Use a plastic or wooden rice paddle and plastic tongs, not metal utensils, to avoid scratching the nonstick surface.
- Before starting to cook, clean the underside of the rice cooker bowl and the surface of the heating plate.
- After using the rice cooker, remove the bowl and wash in hot, soapy water, then rinse and dry completely before returning to the rice cooker.
- If rice has stuck to the bottom of the bowl, fill it with hot, soapy water and let stand for 10 minutes before cleaning.
- Some rice cookers have a detachable lid for easy cleaning. Others have a spoon holder and a condensation cup that attach to the side of the cooker. Remove both attachments, empty any liquid from the cup, then wash and dry the items.
- Using a dry, clean kitchen towel, wipe any condensation from around the inner seal of the lid if it has one (some rice cookers have a lid without a seal).

Troubleshooting

- If the cooker is not working properly, check the rice cooker bowl. It must be properly positioned inside the cooker. To ensure that the bowl is sitting flat on the heating plate, rotate it a few times.

- If the cook button will not stay on in "cook" position when heating oil to brown ingredients before cooking, activate spring loaded heating element.

- If "cook" button turns off before food is browned sufficiently, simply switch it on again. If it still will not stay in "on" position, wait a few minutes and try again.

Steaming in a rice cooker

The advantage of steaming foods is that they generally do not require the use of oil and retain most of their nutritional value. Some rice cookers are designed with one or two steamer trays. Food can be placed in the tray above stock or water, the lid closed and the cooker turned on. If no trays are supplied, a trivet can be put in the bottom of the rice cooker bowl, and the food can be placed on a heatproof plate or bowl and set on the trivet.

Be sure that the steamer tray or trivet does not touch the liquid in the rice cooker bowl. A plate or bowl used with a trivet must allow steam to circulate evenly. Finally, do not let the liquid in the rice cooker bowl boil dry. Liquid can be added during the steaming process, if required; be sure to add hot liquid in order to maintain the proper temperature.

Tips
- Cut foods into uniform sizes for even cooking.
- Smaller pieces steam faster than larger ones.
- Slower-cooking vegetables can be added earlier or cut into smaller pieces than faster-cooking vegetables, for more even cooking.
- Vegetables can be cooked longer than usual if a soft texture is desired. More water should be added to the rice cooker if needed.
- Frozen vegetables do not need to be defrosted before steaming.
- Food should be arranged in a single layer for even cooking.

- As steamed food can look bland, sear meat and poultry before steaming, if desired.
- Place parchment (baking) paper or cabbage or lettuce leaves under dumplings to prevent them from sticking to the steamer tray.
- Seafood and chicken can be wrapped in parchment (baking) paper (see picture below), aluminum foil or blanched leaves, such as banana or bamboo. Cooking food in parcels not only contains the juices, which can be served as a sauce, but also allows individual servings to be seasoned to taste. The parcels are also attractive to serve to guests.
- Timing is based on the thickness of food, not on the weight.
- Do not put the food to be steamed over the liquid until the liquid is simmering. Cooking time starts then.

Steaming cooking guide

A number of variables affect cooking times. Among them are the size and thickness of food and the amount being cooked, whether the steamer is close to or far above the simmering liquid, and whether one or two steamers are used. Since cooking times can vary, always check food after the shortest cooking time. Cooking time for vegetables will depend on preferred crispness.

Seafood
- Fish fillets—5–8 minutes (depending on thickness and texture)
- Fish steaks—8–12 minutes (depending on thickness)
- Mussels, in shell—5–10 minutes
- Clams, in shell—4–8 minutes
- Shrimp (prawns)—4–6 minutes (depending on size)
- Scallops—3–4 minutes
- Lobster tails—12–15 minutes

Chicken
- Breast halves, boneless—12–15 minutes
- Thighs, boneless—15–18 minutes
- Drumsticks, bone in—20–25 minutes

Vegetables
- Asparagus spears—3–5 minutes
- Beans, green—5–7 minutes
- Beets, small whole (3 oz/90 g) —15–20 minutes
- Broccoli, florets—5–8 minutes
- Carrots, thin slices—5–8 minutes
- Potatoes, medium whole (6 oz/180 g) —30–35 minutes
- Potatoes, whole new (4 oz/125 g) —20–25 minutes
- Sweet potatoes (kumeras) (2-inch/5-cm chunks)—15–20 minutes
- Winter squash (pumpkin) (2-inch/5-cm chunks)—15–20 minutes
- Zucchini (courgette), sliced—5 minutes

Types of rice

Brown rice and polished white rice are the two common types used in the kitchen. When brown rice is processed, only the inedible outer husk is removed. The nutritious, high-fiber bran coating is retained and gives the rice a light tan color, a chewy texture and a slightly nutty flavor. Because the bran is not removed, brown rice turns rancid more quickly and takes longer to cook than white. Instant or quick brown or white rice has been fully or partially parboiled, then dehydrated, and cooks in half or less the normal time, but tends to lack flavor and texture. The proportion of Amylopekin and amylose starch content determines moisture of rice amd therefore its cooking quantities.

Rice is classified by its size and shape:

LONG GRAIN The grains, whether brown or white, are four or five times longer than they are wide, with higher amylose starch content. When cooked, they become light and dry and separate easily. This type of rice is ideal for pilafs and rice salads.

MEDIUM GRAIN Shorter and moister than long grain rice, but not as starchy as short grain. The grains are fairly fluffy when cooked, but begin to clump once they start to cool. These properties make the rice suitable for desserts, paella and sushi and for eating with chopsticks.

SHORT GRAIN Plump, almost round grains with a higher amylopectin starch content than long or medium grains. This type is ideal for making desserts and sushi and for eating with chopsticks.

Arborio rice

Basmati rice

Calasparra rice

Glutinous rice

Common varieties of rice

ARBORIO An Italian rice with short to medium grains and a high starch content that gives the cooked rice a creamy texture. The grains swell and absorb a greater amount of liquid than many other rice varieties. Used for risotto and other Mediterranean dishes. Carnaroli super fino, and the slightly smaller Vialone Nano semi fino, similar varieties, are especially well suited for making risotto. Unlike other rice, Arborio is not rinsed before cooking for dishes like risotto as the surface starch adds to the creaminess of the dish.

BASMATI A dry, aromatic, long-grain rice. It benefits from being soaked in water for 30 minutes before cooking or adding slightly more water when cooking. Suited to Indian and Middle Eastern dishes. Texmati is an American variety of basmati grown in Texas.

CALASPARRA A Spanish medium-grain rice, traditionally used for paella. Arborio can be substituted.

GLUTINOUS RICE Short-grain rice with a sticky texture, hence its alternative name, sticky rice. Used in Asian cooking, mainly in desserts and sweets such as Japanese mochi, and sometimes sushi. Soak before cooking.

JASMINE A subtly fragrant, soft, long-grain rice. Commonly used in Asian dishes, especially Thai and Vietnamese.

SUSHI Short or medium grain, and also sold as Nishiki or Koshihikari rice. It is moist and slightly sweet, so in Japan it is not traditionally cooked with salt. Because the cooked grains gently cling together, the rice can be eaten with chopsticks and molded for preparations such as sushi.

THAI BLACK RICE A long-grain rice with a chewy texture and grassy flavor well suited for use in desserts, especially those with coconut milk and fruit. This type benefits from being soaked overnight before cooking. The soluble bran coating leaches into the soaking and cooking liquid, coloring it purple.

Jasmine rice

Sushi rice

Thai black rice

Wild rice

Cooking perfect rice

Whether you use a standard measuring cup or a cooker's rice cup, the preparation for cooking rice is the same. Measure the rice and then rinse it according to the directions in individual recipes. If using a standard measuring cup, measure the water with the same cup. If using a rice cup, put the rice in the rice cooker bowl and add water to the equivalent rice cup measure marked on the inside of the bowl. For example, if you measured 2 rice cups of rice, put rice in cooker, then add water up to the 2 cup level on the bowl.

RINSING RICE   Most rice varieties benefit from being rinsed in cold water until the water runs clear. This removes excess starch so the rice does not become sticky. The exceptions are Arborio and related types, as the starch on the surface of the grains contributes the appealing creaminess characteristic of dishes like risotto.

SOAKING THE RICE   Although it's not essential, some rice varieties, such as basmati and brown rice, should be rinsed and then soaked in water for 30 minutes or more before cooking. Short- or medium-grain rice used for sushi also benefits from soaking, to help ensure uniform cooking and optimum texture.

Tips

- For measuring rice, use the rice cup provided with the rice cooker. Cups may vary with different brands of cookers (see cooking guide, below).
- Always measure rice by filling the cup level with the rim, or level marked on cup. Never use heaping cups.
- Because rice increases in volume as it cooks, never fill the rice cooker beyond its recommended capacity.
- Always cook the minimum quantity of rice recommended by the manufacturer, usually 2 rice cups.
- Once the rice is cooked, open the lid and turn the rice with a rice paddle. Close the lid and leave the rice undisturbed for 10–15 minutes to allow excess moisture to be absorbed. This will result in fluffier, more evenly cooked rice.
- For firmer rice, use slightly less water; for softer rice, add slightly more.
- Certain types of rice, such as Arborio and wild rice blends, may require more liquid than other varieties.
- When cooking large quantities of rice, the amount of water can be decreased slightly. The cooking time will need to be increased slightly (this will happen automatically, if using an electric cooker).
- Rice that is nearing its expiration date may require slightly more water than new-season rice as the grains have lost some of their moisture.

Reheating cooked rice

Put leftover cooked rice in the rice cooker bowl. Add 2–3 tablespoons water or stock, close the lid and activate the "cook" switch. Stir the rice occasionally, adding more water or stock if necessary, and cook until rice is heated through. Push "warm" to keep rice warm until serving.

Cooking guide

Using standard measuring cup

Uncooked amount 1 cup (7 oz/220 g) white rice
Water 1 cup (8 fl oz/250 ml)
Yield About 3 cups (15 oz/470 g)
Cooking Time 15 minutes

Uncooked amount 1 cup (7 oz/220 g) brown rice
Water 1 cup (8 fl oz/250 ml)
Yield About 2½ cups (12 oz/375 g)
Cooking Time 35–40 minutes

Uncooked amount 1 cup (7 oz/220 g) wild rice
Water 1 cup (8 fl oz/250 ml)
Yield About 2½ (12 oz/375 g)
Cooking Time 35–40 minutes

Using rice measuring cup

White rice
Uncooked amount 2 rice cups
Water 2 rice cups
Yield 4 rice cups
Cooking Time 15 minutes

Uncooked amount 4 rice cups
Water 4 rice cups
Yield 8 rice cups
Cooking Time 18 minutes

Uncooked amount 6 rice cups
Water 6 rice cups
Yield 12 rice cups
Cooking Time 22 minutes

Brown rice
Uncooked amount 2 rice cups
Water 3 rice cups
Yield 5 rice cups
Cooking Time 25–30 minutes

Uncooked amount 4 rice cups
Water 6 rice cups
Yield 10 rice cups
Cooking Time 35–40 minutes

Uncooked amount 6 rice cups
Water 9 rice cups
Yield 15 rice cups
Cooking Time 40–45 minutes

WHITE RICE

1¹⁄₂ cups (10¹⁄₂ oz/315 g) long- or short-grain white rice
1¹⁄₂ cups (12 fl oz/375 ml) water
¹⁄₂ teaspoon salt (optional)

Put rice in a bowl with cold water to cover. Gently rub grains together with your fingers to remove any excess surface starch. Drain. Repeat 3 or 4 times until water is nearly clear. Combine rice, water and salt (if using) in rice cooker bowl, spreading rice evenly in bottom of bowl. Close lid and press "cook." Cook until rice cooker turns to "warm," 12–15 minutes. Fluff rice with a rice paddle, close lid and let stand for 10–15 minutes to absorb any remaining moisture.

QUICK RECIPE VARIATIONS

Saffron rice Add 5–10 saffron threads for every 1 cup (8 fl oz/250 ml) water.

Savory rice with herbs Substitute beef, chicken, fish or vegetable stock for water. Stir chopped fresh flat-leaf (Italian) parsley, dill, basil, chives or cilantro (coriander) into cooked rice.

Sweet rice For half of water, substitute fruit juice. Using milk products is not recommended as they will scorch bottom of rice cooker bowl. Instead, stir cream or yogurt into rice after it is cooked. Chopped fresh fruit may also be stirred into hot cooked rice.

BROWN RICE

2 cups (14 oz/440 g) brown rice
3 cups (24 fl oz/750 ml) water or stock
1 teaspoon salt (optional)

Put rice in a bowl with cold water to cover. Gently rub the grains together with your fingers to remove any excess surface starch. Drain. Combine rice, water and salt (if using) in rice cooker bowl, spreading rice evenly in bottom of bowl. If time permits, let stand for 30 minutes before cooking. Close lid and press "cook." Cook until rice cooker turns to "warm," 35–40 minutes. Fluff rice with a rice paddle, close lid and stand for 10–15 minutes to absorb any remaining moisture.

Tip This recipe produces rice with a firm texture. For softer rice, add ¼–½ cup (2–4 fl oz/60–125 ml) more water, depending on preferred texture.

QUICK AND EASY RICE SALADS

Put hot, cooked rice in a large, shallow dish to cool. This also helps keep rice grains separate. Combine warm cooked rice with salad dressing so grains absorb flavor. Cover and refrigerate, then add one of the following combinations:

Cherry tomatoes, halved; English (hothouse) cucumber, sliced; red bell pepper (capsicum), chopped; toasted pine nuts; fresh (flat-leaf) parsley, chopped; scallion (green onion), thinly sliced; strips of smoked chicken.

Sliced or bite-sized grilled vegetables such as zucchini (courgette), red onion and red bell peppers (capsicums); crumbled feta cheese; oil-packed sun-dried tomatoes, drained and cut into thin strips; black olives such as Niçoise or Kalamata.

Orange segments, cut in half; black olives such as Niçoise or Kalamata; thinly sliced red onion; fennel bulb, trimmed and cut into thin strips; cooked shrimp (prawns).

Dried apricots, thinly sliced; toasted almonds or cashews; dried currants; toasted pumpkin seeds; toasted cumin seeds, crushed or left whole; chopped fresh mint; scallions (green onions), thinly sliced; grilled lamb tenderloin, thinly sliced.

Rice

SPICY TOMATO RICE

SERVES 4

1 cup (7 oz/220 g) basmati rice

1 tablespoon canola oil

1 small yellow (brown) onion, chopped

2 cloves garlic, finely chopped

1 red chili pepper such as bird's-eye or Thai, seeded and chopped

1 teaspoon cumin seeds

6 peppercorns

2 whole cloves

1 cinnamon stick

$\frac{1}{2}$ cup (2$\frac{1}{2}$ oz/75 g) fresh or frozen peas

1 cup (6$\frac{1}{2}$ oz/200 g) canned whole tomatoes

2 tablespoons tomato paste

$\frac{1}{2}$ teaspoon salt

1$\frac{3}{4}$ cups (14 fl oz/440 ml) water or stock

2 tablespoons chopped fresh cilantro (coriander)

Put rice in a bowl with cold water to cover. Gently rub grains together with your fingers to remove any excess surface starch. Drain. Return rice to bowl, add cold water to cover and let stand for 5 minutes. Drain and set aside.

Place oil in rice cooker bowl, press "cook" and heat for 1 minute. Add onion, garlic and chili and cook, stirring constantly, until onion is soft, about 2 minutes. Add cumin seeds, peppercorns, cloves and cinnamon stick and cook for 2 minutes. Stir in rice, peas, tomatoes and tomato paste, and cook, stirring constantly, until well combined, about 2 minutes. Add salt and water. Close lid and cook until rice cooker switches to "warm," 12–15 minutes. Stir with a rice paddle, close lid and let stand for 10 minutes on "warm." Using a fork, stir in cilantro. Remove whole cloves and cinnamon stick before serving.

SPICED BROWN RICE

SERVES 4

2 cups (14 oz/440 g) brown rice
2 tablespoons peanut oil
1/4 cup (1 oz/30 g) shallots, thinly sliced
1–2 red chili peppers such as bird's-eye or Thai,
    seeded and finely sliced
1 tablespoon peeled and finely grated fresh ginger
3 1/2 cups (28 fl oz/875 ml) stock or water
1/2 teaspoon salt

Put rice in a bowl with cold water to cover. Gently rub grains together with your fingers to remove any excess surface starch. Drain. Place oil in rice cooker bowl, press "cook" and heat for 1 minute. Add shallots, chilis and ginger and cook, stirring occasionally, until aromatic, 3–4 minutes. Add rice and stir to coat grains with oil. Add stock and salt. Close lid and press "cook." Cook until rice cooker turns to "warm," 35–40 minutes. Fluff rice with a rice paddle, close lid and let stand for 10–15 minutes to absorb any remaining moisture.

MIXED RICE SALAD

SERVES 4–6

1 cup (7 oz/220 g) white rice, rinsed

1 cup (7 oz/220 g) brown rice, rinsed

1/4 cup (1 1/2 oz/45 g) wild rice, rinsed

3 1/2 cups (28 fl oz/875 ml) chicken stock

1 small red onion, halved and thinly sliced

1 1/2 cups (12 oz/375 g) drained oil-packed roasted bell peppers (capsicums), finely sliced, or 1 or 2 fresh red bell peppers, roasted, seeded and finely sliced

6 oz (180 g) snowpeas (mange-tout), trimmed and thinly sliced on the diagonal

3 scallions (green onions), finely sliced

1/3 cup (3 oz/90 g) smoked almonds, coarsely chopped

FOR DRESSING

1/4 cup (2 fl oz/60 ml) olive oil

3 tablespoons red wine vinegar

3 teaspoons Japanese soy sauce

1 teaspoon Asian sesame oil

2 tablespoons sweet chili sauce

Combine rices and stock in rice cooker bowl, spreading rices evenly in bottom of bowl. Close lid and press "cook." Cook until rice cooker turns to "warm," 35–40 minutes. Meanwhile, to make dressing, place all ingredients in a small bowl and whisk to combine. Transfer cooked rice to a bowl. Stir dressing through rice and set aside to cool. Add onion, bell peppers, snowpeas, scallions and nuts, reserving a few for garnish, and toss to combine.

To roast bell peppers Put peppers on a baking sheet in a hot oven (400°F/200°C). Turn occasionally, until skin turns black and blistered. Transfer to a plate and tent with aluminum foil or put in a plastic bag. When peppers are cool enough to handle, remove blackened skin with paper towel, fingers or small paring knife. Remove seeds and ribs.

Tip Add cooked shrimp (prawns), sliced smoked chicken or sliced, grilled, marinated beef.

INDIAN PILAF

SERVES 4

1¼ cups (9 oz/280 g) basmati rice
1 tablespoon canola oil
1 yellow (brown) onion, chopped
2 cloves garlic, finely chopped
1 teaspoon fennel seeds
1 tablespoon sesame seeds
½ teaspoon ground turmeric
1 teaspoon ground cumin
½ teaspoon salt
2 whole cloves
3 cardamom pods, lightly crushed
6 peppercorns
1¾ cups (14 fl oz/440 ml) chicken stock
fresh curry leaves for garnish (optional)

Put rice in a bowl with cold water to cover. Gently rub grains together with your fingers to remove any excess surface starch. Drain. Return rice to bowl, add cold water to cover and let stand for 30 minutes. Drain and set aside.

Place oil in rice cooker bowl, press "cook" and heat for 1 minute. Add onion and garlic and cook, stirring constantly, until onion is soft, about 2 minutes. Stir in fennel seeds, sesame seeds, turmeric, cumin, salt, cloves, cardamom and peppercorns. Cook, stirring constantly, until fragrant, 1–2 minutes. Add rice and cook, stirring constantly, until grains are opaque, about 2 minutes. Pour in stock. Close lid and cook until rice cooker switches to "warm," 12–15 minutes. Stir with a rice paddle, close lid and let stand for 10 minutes on "warm." Garnish with curry leaves, if desired.

SHRIMP FRIED RICE

SERVES 6–8

2 cups (14 oz/440 g) short- or medium-grain white rice
2 cups (8 fl oz/16 ml) water
6 dried black mushrooms
¼ cup (1½ oz/45 g) dried lotus seeds (optional)
3 tablespoons canola oil
3 oz (90 g) spicy pork sausage, removed from casing and diced
1 carrot, peeled and diced
1 lb (500 g) medium shrimp (prawns), shelled, deveined and chopped, reserving 2 whole shrimp for garnish
1 small yellow (brown) onion, diced
2 tablespoons fish sauce
½ teaspoon salt
cracked pepper
⅓ cup (½ oz/15 g) Chinese (garlic) chives, coarsely chopped
fresh cilantro (coriander) sprigs for garnish
1 red chili pepper such as serrano or Thai, seeded and thinly sliced, for garnish

Put rice in a bowl with cold water to cover. Gently rub grains together with your fingers to remove any excess surface starch. Drain. Combine rice and water in rice cooker bowl, spreading rice evenly in bottom of bowl. Close the lid and press "cook." Cook until rice cooker turns to "warm," 12–15 minutes. Transfer rice to a bowl, cover and keep warm.

Meanwhile, place mushrooms in a small bowl with hot water to cover and soak for 20 minutes. Drain and squeeze mushrooms to remove all liquid. Cut off and discard tough stems and dice caps. If using lotus seeds, soak in warm water to cover for 20 minutes. Insert a toothpick in seeds from end to end to remove any bitter green sprouts. Cook seeds in boiling water for 20 minutes. Drain.

Place half the oil in rice cooker bowl, press "cook" and heat for 1 minute. Working in batches, add sausage, mushrooms, lotus seeds, carrot, shrimp and onion, and cook, stirring constantly, until onion softens and shrimp turn pink, about 5 minutes. Remove whole shrimp and set aside for garnish. Stir in fish sauce, salt, pepper to taste and all but 1 tablespoon chives.

Lightly oil a 2-qt (2-L) bowl or eight 1-cup (8–fl oz/250-ml) ramekins. Fill bowl or each ramekin one-third full with cooked rice, pressing in place. Spread evenly with sausage mixture, then cover with remaining rice. Press to compact layers firmly, then unmold onto a plate. If using a bowl, cut each remaining whole shrimp in half lengthwise. If using ramekins, cut each into 4 pieces. Garnish rice with shrimp, cilantro sprigs and chili slices.

PAELLA

SERVES 4

2 tablespoons olive oil

1 red onion, diced

2 cloves garlic, crushed

1 chorizo sausage, removed from casing and sliced

1/2 teaspoon smoked paprika or 1 teaspoon sweet or
hot paprika

2 cups (14 oz/440 g) Arborio or long-grain rice, rinsed

3/4 lb (12 oz/375 g) skinless, boneless chicken thighs,
cut into 2-inch (5-cm) pieces

1 can (14 oz/440 g) canned whole tomatoes

3 cups (24 fl oz/750 ml) chicken stock, plus more if
needed

1 teaspoon salt

1 teaspoon saffron threads soaked in 1/4 cup
(2 fl oz/60 ml) boiling water

3/4 lb (12 oz/375 g) medium shrimp (prawns), peeled
and deveined

8 mussels, scrubbed and debearded

about 8 oz (250 g) calamari, cleaned and thinly sliced,
or 6 oz (180 g) calamari tubes, thinly sliced
crosswise, optional

1 red bell pepper (capsicum), roasted (page 23),
peeled, seeded and thinly sliced

1 cup (5 oz/150 g) fresh or frozen peas

1 lemon, cut into 6 wedges

Place oil in rice cooker bowl, press "cook" and
heat for 1 minute. Add onion, garlic and
chorizo and cook, stirring occasionally, until
onion softens slightly, about 2 minutes. Stir in
paprika and rice and cook, stirring constantly,
until grains are opaque, about 2 minutes. Add
chicken, tomatoes, stock, salt and saffron, and
stir to combine. Close lid and press "cook."
Cook for 15 minutes. Stir in seafood, bell
pepper and peas. Close lid and cook until rice
cooker switches to "warm," 5–10 minutes. Add
more stock or water if rice needs further
cooking or if softer rice is desired. Close lid
and let stand for 10 minutes or longer if drier
texture is desired. Serve with lemon wedges
scattered on top.

LEMON-DILL RISOTTO

SERVES 4

2 tablespoons olive oil

1 clove garlic, crushed

1 leek, sliced crosswise

1½ cups (10½ oz/315 g) Arborio rice

½ cup (4 fl oz/125 ml) dry white wine

2–3 cups (16–24 fl oz/500–750 ml) vegetable or
   chicken stock

½ teaspoon salt

cracked pepper

½ cup (2 oz/60 g) grated Parmesan cheese

1–2 tablespoons lemon juice

1 teaspoon finely grated lemon zest

2 tablespoons chopped fresh dill

Place oil in rice cooker bowl, press "cook" and heat for 1 minute. Add garlic and leek and cook, stirring constantly, until leeks begin to soften, about 5 minutes. Add rice and stir to coat with oil. Add wine, stock, salt and pepper to taste. Close lid and press "cook." Cook until cooker switches to "warm," 15–20 minutes, stirring halfway through cooking time with a rice paddle. Stir rice, then fold in cheese, lemon juice and zest. Close lid and let stand for 10 minutes on "warm." Garnish with dill before serving.

Tip Cook diced chicken with the rice or add mixed seafood such as shrimp (prawns), mussels and calamari to the rice for the last 5 minutes of cooking.

SUSHI RICE

MAKES 6 CUPS (30 oz/940 g)

1½ cups (10 ½ oz/315 g) short-grain or sushi rice such
    as Koshihikari or Nishiki, rinsed
1½ cups (12 fl oz/375 ml) water
3 tablespoons rice vinegar
2 tablespoons sugar
¾ teaspoon salt

Combine rice and water in rice cooker bowl,
spreading rice evenly in bottom of bowl. Close
lid and press "cook." Cook until cooker
switches to "warm," 12–15 minutes. Stir rice
with a rice paddle, close lid and let stand for
10 minutes on "warm." Transfer rice to a large,
shallow glass or ceramic dish. Heat vinegar,
sugar and salt in a small saucepan over low
heat until sugar dissolves. Pour vinegar mixture
over rice and, holding a plastic or wooden rice
spatula at a 45-degree angle, slice through rice
to break up lumps and evenly distribute
vinegar mixture. Spread rice out and let cool
to room temperature. Cover with a damp
kitchen towel to prevent rice from drying out
until ready to use.

CHIRASHI SUSHI

SERVES 4

Divide Sushi Rice among 4 bowls. On rice
arrange a selection of ingredients:

thinly sliced smoked salmon, sashimi tuna or
salmon; sliced English (hothouse) cucumber
and avocado; thin asparagus spears, blanched
and sliced on the diagonal into 2-inch (5-cm)
pieces; blanched snowpeas (mange-tout).
Accompany with wasabi, slices of pink pickled
ginger (gari) and Japanese soy sauce.

WILD RICE

SERVES 4

Not a true rice, wild rice refers to the seeds of an aquatic grass. The longer the seeds, the more highly prized and the more expensive. The seeds are heated and partially hulled after harvest. This process and the length of the seeds affects the amount of water and the cooking time required. In general, wild rice takes longer to cook than conventional rice. Its unique nutty taste and chewy texture make it ideal for combining with other types of rice or with barley.

2 cups (14 oz/440 g) wild rice
3 cups (24 fl oz/750 ml) stock or water
½ teaspoon salt (optional)

Combine wild rice, stock and salt (if using) in rice cooker bowl, spreading rice evenly in bottom of bowl. Close lid and press "cook." Cook until cooker turns to "warm," about 40 minutes. Fluff rice with a rice paddle, close lid and let stand for 10–15 minutes to absorb any remaining moisture.

Tip Stir sautéed mushrooms, chopped garlic and chopped fresh thyme and flat-leaf (Italian) parsley into rice. Use as basis of a salad tossed with your favorite dressing and with nuts and fresh or dried fruit.

Other grains

CINNAMON-APPLE OATMEAL

SERVES 3–4

1 cup (3 oz/90 g) rolled oats
1½ cups (12 fl oz/375 ml) apple or orange juice
¾ cup (6 fl oz/180 ml) water
pinch salt (optional)
⅓ cup (2 oz/60 g) mixed dried fruit such as golden
  raisins (sultanas), chopped apples and chopped
  apricots
½ teaspoon ground cinnamon or nutmeg
½ cup (4 oz/125 g) plain or fruit-flavored yogurt

Combine oats, juice, water, salt (if using) and fruit in rice cooker bowl, spreading ingredients evenly on bottom of bowl. Close lid and press "cook." Cook, stirring once halfway through cooking, until oats and fruit are soft, 12–15 minutes. Let stand on "warm" with lid closed for 10 minutes if a softer texture is desired. Stir in cinnamon and yogurt or serve yogurt on side.

Tip Substitute fresh fruit such as whole fresh berries or sliced peaches or bananas for dried fruit.

MILLET

Millet has been a staple in Africa and Asia for centuries. The indigestible hull is removed from the round grains, making them cook fairly quickly and producing fluffy grains with a mild, delicate flavor. Millet benefits from being lightly toasted, with or without butter or oil. It combines well with other grains.

1 tablespoon unsalted butter
1 tablespoon olive oil
1 cup (6 oz/180 g) millet, rinsed
2 cups (16 fl oz/500 ml) stock or water
½ teaspoon salt

Put butter and oil in rice cooker bowl and press "cook." When butter is melted, add millet and cook, stirring constantly, until toasted and golden, about 3 minutes. Add stock and salt. Close lid and cook until rice cooker switches to "warm," 25–30 minutes. Let stand for 5 minutes on "warm" with lid closed before serving as a rice or oat substitute.

BARLEY

1 cup (6½ oz/200 g) pearl barley, rinsed
2 cups (16 fl oz/500 ml) stock or water
½ teaspoon salt

Combine barley, stock and salt in rice cooker bowl, spreading barley evenly over bottom of bowl. Close lid and press "cook." Cook until rice cooker switches to "warm," about 35 minutes. Fluff with a rice paddle, close lid and let stand for 10 minutes to absorb any remaining liquid. Serve as a rice substitute.

Tip Substitute half the stock or water with fruit juice and serve topped with fresh fruit.

BARLEY AND MUSHROOM RISOTTO

SERVES 3 OR 4

1 oz (30 g) dried porcini mushrooms
1 tablespoon unsalted butter
1 tablespoon olive oil
1 large yellow (brown) onion, chopped
1 clove garlic, crushed
1 cup (6½ oz/200 g) pearl barley
¾ cup (6 fl oz/180 ml) white wine
4 cups (32 fl oz/1 L) vegetable or chicken stock, plus
    more if needed

½ teaspoon salt
cracked pepper
5 oz (150 g) fresh shiitake mushrooms, stems removed
    and caps sliced
1 cup (2 oz/60 g) chopped fresh spinach
grated zest and juice of 1 lemon
½ cup (2 oz/60 g) grated Parmesan cheese

Soak porcini mushrooms in a small bowl with 1 cup (8 fl oz/250 ml) boiling water for 30 minutes. Drain and chop. Put butter and oil in rice cooker bowl and press "cook." When butter is melted, add onion and garlic and cook, stirring occasionally, until onion softens slightly, about 2 minutes. Add barley and stir to coat with oil. Pour in wine and stir stock, salt and pepper to taste. Close lid and cook, stirring occasionally, until rice cooker switches to "warm," 55–60 minutes. Add more stock, close lid and cook longer if a softer texture is desired. Stir in porcini and shiitake mushrooms, spinach and lemon zest and juice, close lid and cook until heated through, about 5 minutes. Accompany with Parmesan cheese.

SPLIT PEA, CUMIN AND GARLIC DIP WITH VEGETABLES AND LAVOSH

SERVES 4–6

2 teaspoons cumin seeds

1 tablespoon olive oil plus ¼ cup (2 fl oz/60 ml)

1 yellow (brown) onion, chopped

2 cloves garlic, crushed

1 cup (7 oz/220 g) yellow split peas, rinsed

¼ cup (2 fl oz/60 ml) lemon juice

1 red chili pepper such as serrano, seeded and finely chopped (optional)

salt and cracked pepper

½ cup (3 oz/90 g) finely diced red bell pepper (capsicum)

¼ cup (⅓ oz/10 g) chopped fresh cilantro (coriander) or flat-leaf (Italian) parsley

FOR SERVING

¼ lb (125 g) snowpeas (mange-tout), trimmed and blanched

12 thin asparagus spears, ends trimmed, blanched and cut into 3-inch (7.5-cm) lengths

¼ lb (125 g) green beans, trimmed and blanched

8–12 pieces lavosh

Turn rice cooker to "cook" and heat for 1 minute. Add cumin seeds and toast, stirring constantly, until aromatic, about 2 minutes. Remove and set aside. Add 1 tablespoon oil and heat for 1 minute. Add onion and garlic and cook, stirring occasionally, until onion softens slightly, 2–3 minutes. Add split peas and enough water to cover them. Close lid and press "cook." Cook until beans are tender and beginning to break down, and rice cooker switches to "warm," about 30 minutes. Drain and let cool. Puree pea mixture in a food processor. With motor running, gradually add ¼ cup oil, then lemon juice, cumin seeds, chili and salt and pepper to taste. Transfer dip to a bowl and stir in bell pepper and cilantro. Serve with snowpeas, asparagus, green beans and lavosh.

Tip Dip can also be served as an accompaniment to main meals.

CANNELLINI, SPINACH AND YOGURT DIP WITH SESAME TOASTS

SERVES 4–6

1 cup (7 oz/220 g) dried cannellini beans, rinsed

about 3 cups (24 fl oz/750 ml) vegetable or chicken
   stock or water

1 cup (7 oz/220 g) chopped, blanched spinach

3 tablespoons lime juice

2 cloves garlic, crushed

2 teaspoons ground cumin

1 cup (8 oz/250 g) thick plain yogurt

1/3 cup (2 oz/60 g) chopped drained oil-packed sun-
   dried tomatoes

salt and cracked pepper

FOR SESAME TOASTS

4 pita breads, cut into wedges

1 egg white, lightly beaten

1/3 cup (1 1/2 oz/45 g) sesame seeds

1/3 cup (1 1/2 oz/45 g) grated Parmesan cheese

Put cannellini beans in rice cooker bowl. Add enough stock to cover beans. Close lid and press "cook." Cook until beans are tender, about 45 minutes. Drain and let cool.

Meanwhile, make sesame toasts: Preheat oven to 350°F (180°C/gas mark 4). Arrange pita wedges on a baking sheet and brush lightly with egg white. Sprinkle half of wedges with sesame seeds and other half with cheese. Bake until lightly browned and crisp, about 10 minutes. Toasts can be prepared ahead and stored in an airtight container for up to 1 week.

Puree beans and spinach in a food processor. With motor running, add lime juice, garlic and cumin. Transfer dip to a bowl and stir in yogurt and tomatoes and season with salt and pepper. Serve with sesame toasts.

Tip Canned cannellini beans can be used in this recipe. Do not cook the cannellini beans, simply rinse and puree.

Pasta and **noodles**

TOMATO-BASIL PASTA

SERVES 4–6

1 tablespoon olive oil

2 cloves garlic, crushed

1 red chili pepper such as serrano, seeded and finely
   chopped (optional)

1 yellow (brown) onion, chopped

¾ lb (375 g) farfalle or fusilli

3 cups (24 fl oz/750 ml) hot vegetable or chicken stock

1 can (14 oz/440 g) whole tomatoes

2 tablespoons tomato paste

2 tablespoons Worcestershire sauce

½ cup (¾ oz/20 g) chopped fresh basil

salt and cracked pepper

⅓ cup (2 oz/60 g) small pitted black olives such as
   Nicoise or Kalamata, sliced

Put oil in rice cooker bowl, press "cook" and heat for 1 minute. Add garlic, chili and onion and cook, stirring occasionally, until onion softens slightly, about 2 minutes. Add pasta, stock, tomatoes, tomato paste, Worcestershire sauce, ⅓ cup basil, and salt and pepper to taste. Close lid and press "cook." Cook, stirring occasionally, until pasta is al dente, about 10 minutes. Stir in olives, garnish with remaining fresh basil leaves and serve.

Tip Bringing liquid to a boil before adding pasta or noodles helps prevent them sticking together. Alternatively, preheat the liquid before pouring into the rice cooker bowl.

To make seafood pasta Steam mussels, peeled and deveined shrimp (prawns), sliced calamari or a mixture of shellfish in steamer tray above pasta according to cooking time required. Serve on top of cooked pasta or stir in with olives.

To make beef or chicken pasta Sauté ground (minced) beef or chicken until brown. Add to rice cooker with pasta.

SOBA NOODLES AND CHILI SHRIMP

SERVES 4

1½ lb (750 g) medium shrimp (prawns), peeled and
    deveined
⅓ cup (3 fl oz/90 ml) chili pepper jam
2½ cups (20 fl oz/625 ml) hot water or stock
10 oz (300 g) soba noodles
2 teaspoons Asian sesame oil
¼ lb (4 oz/125 g) snowpeas (mange-tout), thinly
    sliced on diagonal
1 red bell pepper (capsicum), seeded and thinly sliced
3 scallions (green onions), thinly sliced
2 tablespoons chopped fresh cilantro (coriander)
1 tablespoon sesame seeds, toasted in a dry frying
    pan until golden

In a bowl, toss shrimp with half of chili pepper jam. Put water in rice cooker bowl, close lid and press "cook." When water comes to a boil, add shrimp, noodles, oil and remaining jam. Close lid and cook until most of liquid is absorbed, about 4 minutes. Stir in snowpeas, bell pepper and scallions. Close lid and press "cook." Cook until noodles are al dente, 1–2 minutes. Serve garnished with cilantro and sesame seeds.

Tip Substitute sliced calamari, mussels in or out of shell or other quick-cooking seafood for shrimp. Seafood can also be cooked in steamer rack above noodles.

CHICKEN AND HOKKEIN NOODLE SOUP

SERVES 4

1 whole chicken, 4–5 lb (2–2.5 kg)

1 yellow (brown) onion, chopped

2 cloves garlic, crushed

2 bay leaves

8 cups (64 fl oz/2 L) chicken stock

3/4 lb (440 g) fresh hokkien or other 3/8-inch (1-cm)
    wide noodles such as udon, rinsed in warm water

1 cup (5 oz/150 g) fresh or frozen peas

2 carrots, peeled and thinly sliced lengthwise

salt and cracked pepper

2 tablespoons chopped fresh flat-leaf (Italian) parsley

crusty bread for serving

Cut chicken into serving pieces: 2 half breasts, 2 thighs, 2 drumsticks and 2 wings, with wing tips removed. Remove skin from chicken pieces and discard. Reserve back for another use. Put chicken pieces, onion, garlic, bay leaves and stock in rice cooker bowl. Close lid and press "cook." Bring to a boil and cook for 40 minutes. Remove chicken from pot and pull meat off bones. Set aside and keep warm. Add noodles, peas, carrots and chicken to rice cooker bowl. Press "cook" and cook until heated through, about 5 minutes. Remove bay leaves and discard. Season with salt and pepper. Serve garnished with parsley and accompanied with crusty bread.

Tip For a quick soup, rather than cook a whole chicken, purchase a barbecued chicken. Discard skin, remove meat from bones and shred, then stir into liquid with vegetables.

EASY CHICKEN LAKSA

SERVES 4

2 cups (16 fl oz/500 ml) coconut milk

⅓ cup (3 oz/ 90 g) laksa paste or Thai curry paste

2 cups (16 fl oz/500 ml) chicken stock

1 lb (500 g) skinless, boneless chicken breasts or
thighs, thinly sliced

2 tablespoons lime juice

1½ tablespoons fish sauce

1 teaspoon palm sugar (optional)

1 lb (500 g) fresh rice or hokkien noodles, rinsed in hot
water

¼ lb (125 g) bean sprouts

¼ cup (⅓ oz/10 g) chopped fresh cilantro (coriander)

¼ cup (⅓ oz/10 g) chopped fresh mint

Put ½ cup (4 fl oz/125 ml) coconut milk and laksa paste in rice cooker bowl and press "cook." Cook, stirring constantly, for 2 minutes. Add remaining coconut milk, stock and chicken. Close lid and bring to a boil. Cook until chicken is opaque, 5–10 minutes. Stir in lime juice and fish sauce. Taste and add sugar if desired. Put noodles in large soup bowls, add chicken soup and garnish with bean sprouts, cilantro and mint.

Tips

- Substitute 1 lb (500 g) shrimp (prawns), peeled and deveined for chicken, or use ½ lb (250 g) each chicken and shrimp.
- If fresh rice noodles not readily available, substitute with ½ lb (250 g) dried noodles. Pour boiling water over noodles and stand for 5 minutes or until soft. Drain.

Meat

TACOS

SERVES 4

2 tablespoons canola oil

1 large red onion, finely chopped

2 cloves garlic, crushed

1 red chili pepper such as serrano, seeded and finely
   chopped

1 lb (500 g) ground (minced) beef or chicken

1/2 cup (4 fl oz/125 ml) tomato paste

1/2 cup (4 fl oz/125 ml) beef or chicken stock or water

2 tablespoons balsamic vinegar

1 can (14 oz/440 g) whole tomatoes with juice

1 teaspoon sugar

1/2 teaspoon salt

2 teaspoons paprika

2 teaspoons ground cumin

2 teaspoons ground coriander

FOR SERVING

12 taco shells or soft corn tortillas

1/2 head iceberg lettuce, shredded

2 tomatoes, finely diced

3/4 lb (375 g) cheddar cheese, grated

1 small avocado, peeled and diced

Place 1 tablespoon oil in rice cooker bowl, press "cook" and heat for 1 minute. Add onion, garlic and chili and cook until onion softens slightly, about 3 minutes. Remove and set aside. Add remaining oil to rice cooker bowl and, working in batches, cook meat, stirring to break up lumps, until browned, 5–6 minutes. Remove meat and pour oil from bowl. Return bowl to cooker and add onion mixture, meat, tomato paste, stock, vinegar, tomatoes, salt, paprika, cumin and coriander. Stir well to combine. Close lid and press "cook." Cook, stirring occasionally, for 10 minutes. Switch to "warm" and let stand until ready to transfer to a large bowl, or take cooker directly to table. Serve with taco shells, lettuce, tomatoes, cheese and avocado, and let diners assemble their own tacos.

CARAMELIZED SPARERIBS, ASPARAGUS AND BABY POTATOES

SERVES 4

1 tablespoon peanut or corn oil

1½ lb (750 g) beef or pork spareribs

½ cup (4 fl oz/125 ml) hoisin sauce

¾ cup (6 fl oz/180 ml) beef or chicken stock or water,
plus more if needed

1–2 red chili peppers such as Thai or serrano, seeded
and thinly sliced, optional

½ teaspoon Chinese five spice powder

1 lb (500 g) baby potatoes

2 bunches asparagus, 6–7 oz (180–220 g) each, ends
trimmed and spears cut in half

¼ cup (⅓ oz/10 g) chopped fresh cilantro (coriander)
or flat-leaf (Italian) parsley

2 scallions (green onions), thinly sliced

Place oil in rice cooker bowl, press "cook" and heat for 1 minute. Working in batches, cook spareribs, turning occasionally, until browned, 5–6 minutes. Transfer to paper towels to drain. Pour oil from rice cooker bowl. Return bowl to cooker and add spareribs, hoisin sauce, stock, five spice powder, and chili if using. Close lid and press "cook." Cook for 15 minutes, turning ribs occasionally so they do not burn. Scatter potatoes on top of meat. Close lid and cook for 10 minutes; carefully turn meat and potatoes occasionally, so they brown evenly and do not burn. Put asparagus spears in a steamer tray and place above meat, or lay spears over meat. Add more stock or water if needed. Close lid and cook until asparagus is tender but still firm, 3–5 minutes. Remove ribs and vegetables from cooker. Skim oil from cooking liquid and spoon liquid over ribs. Garnish with cilantro and scallions.

BEEF WITH CANNELLINI BEANS AND HORSERADISH CREAM

SERVES 4

2 cups (16 fl oz/500 ml) dry red wine

2 cloves garlic, crushed

3/4 lb (375 g) beef fillet, cut in half lengthwise

1 tablespoon olive oil

1 1/2 cups (12 fl oz/375 ml) beef stock or water

1 cup (7 oz/220 g) dried cannellini beans

3 large tomatoes or 1 can (14 oz/440 g) whole
   tomatoes

1 yellow (brown) onion, cut into thin wedges

1 tablespoon balsamic vinegar

1 teaspoon salt

FOR HORSERADISH CREAM

1 1/2 tablespoons prepared horseradish

1 cup (8 oz/250 g) crème fraîche or thick plain yogurt

1–2 teaspoons lemon or lime juice

salt to taste

In a glass or ceramic bowl, combine 1/4 cup
(2 fl oz/60 ml) red wine and garlic. Add beef,
turn to coat, cover and marinate at room
temperature for 30 minutes. Meanwhile, make
horseradish cream: In a bowl, stir together all
ingredients. Cover and set aside.

Drain beef, reserving marinade. Place oil in
rice cooker bowl, press "cook" and heat for
2 minutes. Add beef and cook for 3–4 minutes
on each side, or longer if well-done beef is
desired. Remove and set aside. Put remaining
red wine, reserved marinade, stock, beans,
tomatoes, onion, vinegar and salt in rice
cooker bowl. Stir to combine, close lid and
press "cook." Cook, stirring occasionally, for
35 minutes. Set beef across beans, close lid and
cook until beans are tender, 5–10 minutes.
Remove beef, tent with aluminum foil and let
stand for 5 minutes. Slice beef across grain.
Serve on top of beans, accompanied with
horseradish cream.

LAMB WITH BARLEY AND CHICKPEAS

SERVES 4

1 lb (500 g) lamb tenderloin, cut in half crosswise

2 teaspoons ground cumin

1 teaspoon ground cinnamon

2 tablespoons ghee or canola oil

1 yellow (brown) onion, cut into thin wedges

2 cloves garlic, crushed

1/2 cup (2 oz/60 g) dried chickpeas (garbanzo beans)

4 cups (32 fl oz/1 L) chicken or vegetable stock, plus more if needed

1 teaspoon salt

1 cup (6½ oz/200 g) pearl barley

1/2 cup (3 oz/90 g) mixed dried fruit such as dark raisins, golden raisins (sultanas) and chopped apples

1/2 cup (3 oz/90 g) whole pistachios or slivered almonds, toasted

1/3 cup (3 oz/90 g) thick plain yogurt

1 tablespoon chopped fresh mint

Rub lamb with half of cumin and cinnamon and set aside. Put 1 tablespoon ghee in rice cooker bowl, press "cook" and heat for 1 minute. Add onion and garlic and cook, stirring occasionally, until onion softens slightly, about 2 minutes. Add chickpeas, stock and salt. Close lid and cook for 10 minutes. Stir in barley, fruit and remaining cumin and cinnamon. Close lid and cook until barley and chickpeas are tender, about 35 minutes. If rice cooker turns to "warm," add more stock if needed and press "cook." Transfer barley mixture to a serving bowl, cover and keep warm.

Wipe rice cooker bowl with paper towels and return bowl to cooker. Add remaining ghee, press "cook" and heat for 1 minute. Add lamb and cook for 3–4 minutes on each side, or longer if lamb is thick or if well-done lamb is desired. Remove, tent with aluminum foil and let stand for 5 minutes. Slice lamb across grain. Serve on top of barley mixture, garnished with pistachios, a dollop of yogurt and chopped mint.

Poultry

DUCK WITH ASIAN GREENS

SERVES 4

½ cup (4 fl oz/125 ml) hoisin sauce
grated zest and juice of 1 orange
½ teaspoon Chinese five spice powder
1 red chili pepper such as Thai or serrano, seeded and
    thinly sliced
4 duck breasts, about 6 oz (180 g) each
1 teaspoon peanut or corn oil
1½ cups (12 fl oz/375 ml) water
2 bunches choy sum, bok choy or other Asian green
    leafy vegetable, 1¼–1½ lb (625–750 g) total,
    trimmed and cut into 4-inch (10-cm) lengths
¼ cup (⅓ oz/10 g) chopped fresh cilantro (coriander)
    leaves
2 scallions (green shallots), chopped
1 teaspoon sesame seeds, toasted in a dry frying pan
    until golden

In a glass or ceramic bowl, stir together hoisin sauce, orange zest and juice, five spice powder and chili. Add duck breasts, turn to coat, cover and marinate, turning occasionally, for 30 minutes. Drain duck, reserving marinade. Place oil in rice cooker bowl, press "cook" and heat for 1 minute. Working in batches if necessary, add duck and cook until browned, 2–3 minutes. Remove duck, pour oil from bowl and return bowl to cooker. Line a steamer tray with parchment (baking) paper. Put duck and reserved marinade on prepared steamer tray. Add water to cooker bowl, close lid and press "cook." When water comes to a boil, place steamer in cooker. Close lid and press "cook." Cook until duck is tender and juices run clear when knife is inserted into thickest part away from bone, 20–25 minutes. Remove duck, tent with aluminum foil and keep warm. Press "cook" and add more water to bowl if necessary. When water is boiling, add greens and cook until wilted, about 2 minutes. Serve duck on greens, garnished with cilantro, scallions and sesame seeds.

MISO SOUP WITH CHICKEN DUMPLINGS

SERVES 4–6

8 cups (64 fl oz/2 L) water

¾ cup (6 fl oz/180 ml) Japanese soy sauce

⅔ cup (5 fl oz/150 ml) mirin or sake

1 tablespoon sugar

1 lb (500 g) ground (minced) chicken

1 tablespoon shiro miso

1 egg, lightly beaten

2 tablepoons all-purpose (plain) flour

1–2 tablespoons pickled ginger, chopped, plus pickled
   ginger for garnish

3 scallions (green onions), finely shredded

1 tablespoon sesame seeds, toasted in a dry frying
   pan until golden

Put water, soy sauce, mirin and sugar in rice cooker. Close lid, press "cook" and bring to a simmer. In a bowl, stir together chicken, miso, egg, flour and chopped ginger. Using 2 spoons or dampened hands, shape chicken mixture into 1-inch (2.5-cm) balls. Place balls in simmering liquid. Stir once to make sure balls are not sticking together. Close lid, press "cook" and cook until a dumpling is no longer pink in center, about 5 minutes. Cook in 2 batches if using a small rice cooker. Serve in bowls, garnished with pickled ginger, scallions and sesame seeds.

Tip Dumplings can be served hot or cold as finger food, accompanied by sweet chili or plum dipping sauce.

To make chicken dumplings and rice

Remove cooked dumplings from rice cooker and keep warm. Remove half of soup (refrigerate or freeze and use in another soup or in a sauce). Combine 3 tablespoons cornstarch (cornflour) with ⅓ cup (3 fl oz/ 90 ml) water and stir into hot liquid. Cook, uncovered, over low heat until a thick, clear sauce forms. Serve with steamed rice and pickled ginger.

MARSALA CHICKEN WITH MANGO AND HAZELNUTS

SERVES 4

1 tablespoon olive oil

1 clove garlic, crushed

1 teaspoon peeled and grated fresh ginger

1 leek or yellow (brown) onion, diced

1½ lb (750 g) boneless, skinless chicken thighs, cut
   into 1-inch (2.5-cm) dice

½ cup (4 fl oz/125 ml) chicken stock

½ cup (4 fl oz/125 ml) marsala

1 teaspoon Chinese five spice powder or allspice

1 tablespoon balsamic vinegar

½ red bell pepper (capsicum), seeded and diced

1 large mango, peeled and pitted, then cut into 1-inch
   (2.5-cm) cubes

2 tablespoons cornstarch (cornflour) dissolved
   in ¼ cup (2 fl oz/60 ml) water

rice (pages 18–19) or potatoes (page 13) for serving

¼ cup (1½ oz/45 g) hazelnuts (filberts), toasted and
   coarsely chopped

Place oil in rice cooker bowl, press "cook" and heat 1 for minute. Add garlic, ginger and leek and cook, stirring occasionally, until leeks soften slightly, 3–4 minutes. Add chicken, stock, marsala, five spice powder and vinegar. Close lid and cook for 12 minutes. Stir in bell pepper and mango, then cornstarch mixture. Press "cook" and cook, uncovered, until sauce thickens and chicken is opaque, about 5 minutes. Serve with potatoes or rice, garnished with hazelnuts.

Tip To toast hazelnuts, place in a baking pan and toast at 350°F (180° C/gas mark 4) until fragrant and beginning to change color, 10–15 minutes. When nuts are cool enough to handle, place in a kitchen towel and rub gently to remove most of skins.

Tip If you have a steamer tray, place baby or diced potatoes on tray and set above chicken to cook for 10–15 minutes, depending on size. Brown potatoes in rice cooker before cooking chicken.

ROSEMARY CHICKEN WITH MASHED POTATOES

SERVES 4

4 skinless, boneless chicken breast halves, 6–7 oz
(180–200 g) each
1 tablespoon Japanese soy sauce
1 tablespoon olive oil
1 large leek, sliced crosswise
2 teaspoons unsalted butter, cut into 4 pieces
⅓ cup (3 fl oz/90 ml) dry white wine
1 cup (6 oz/180 g) Greek-style green olives, pitted and
chopped
¼ cup (⅓ oz/10 g) fresh rosemary leaves
1½ cups (12 fl oz/375 ml) chicken stock
1¼ lb (20 oz/600 g) potatoes such as Desiree or
Yukon gold, peeled and cut into 2-inch (5-cm)
pieces
2–3 tablespoons unsalted butter or ½ cup
(4 fl oz/125 ml) heavy (double) cream
2 tablespoons salted small capers, rinsed and drained

Place chicken in a bowl, drizzle with soy sauce and turn to coat. Put oil in rice cooker bowl, press "cook" and heat for 1 minute. Working in batches, add chicken and cook until browned, about 5 minutes. Cut four 12-inch (30-cm) squares of parchment (baking) paper or aluminum foil. Place leeks in center, dividing evenly. Put a chicken breast on top of leeks. Top each with a piece of butter. Evenly drizzle with wine and top with olives and rosemary. Bring 2 opposite sides of paper over chicken and fold twice to seal. Twist ends of parcel to close securely.

Pour stock in bottom of rice cooker bowl. Place parcels on a steamer tray (or on a plate on top of a trivet) over stock. Close lid, press "cook" and cook for 10 minutes. Remove steamer tray and add potatoes to stock. Return tray to cooker. Cook until juices run clear when a knife is inserted in thickest part of chicken breast and potatoes are tender, about 15 minutes. Transfer potatoes to a bowl and mash. Stir in butter and capers. Serve chicken and leeks on top of mashed potatoes, drizzled with juices in each parcel.

Tip Before cooking the chicken, cut a horizontal pocket in each chicken breast, fill with herbs, leeks and olives and seal with 1 or 2 toothpicks.

HONEY-SOY CHICKEN WITH MACADAMIA-ORANGE COUSCOUS

SERVES 4

3 tablespoons Japanese soy sauce

1 tablespoon honey

1 teaspoon Asian sesame oil

1 teaspoon peeled and grated fresh ginger

1/4 teaspoon star anise or cinnamon powder

12 drumsticks or 4 whole legs, about 3 lb (1.5 kg) total

1 tablespoon olive oil

3/4 cup (6 fl oz/180 ml) chicken stock

1 tablespoon cornstarch (cornflour) dissolved in
   2 tablespoons water (optional)

FOR COUSCOUS

1 1/2 cups (9 oz/280 g) instant couscous

1 1/2 cups (12 fl oz/375 ml) orange juice

2 teaspoons grated orange zest

1–2 tablespoons butter, melted

1/4 cup (1/3 oz/10 g) chopped fresh flat-leaf (Italian)
   parsley

1/4 cup (1 1/2 oz/45 g) macadamia nuts, toasted and
   coarsely chopped

In a glass or ceramic bowl, stir together soy sauce, honey, sesame oil, ginger and star anise powder. Add chicken pieces, turn to coat, cover and marinate, turning occasionally, for at least 30 minutes. Place olive oil in rice cooker bowl, press "cook" and heat for 1 minute. Drain chicken, reserving marinade. Working in batches, cook chicken pieces until lightly browned, about 5 minutes. Remove and set aside. Pour off fat and wipe rice cooker bowl with paper towels. Return bowl to rice cooker and add chicken, stock and reserved marinade. Close lid, press "cook" and cook, turning occasionally, until chicken is opaque, 20–30 minutes, depending on thickness.

Meanwhile, make couscous: Place couscous in a heatproof bowl. In a saucepan over medium-high heat, bring orange juice to a boil. Pour over couscous and let stand for 5 minutes. Fluff with a fork and stir in zest, melted butter, parsley and nuts.

Serve chicken on top of couscous, and drizzle with cooking liquid. Alternatively, remove chicken meat from bones, stir into liquid and serve over couscous. If a thicker sauce is desired, remove chicken and add cornstarch mixture to cooking liquid. Cook, uncovered, over low heat until thickened.

Seafood

RED WINE, TOMATO AND HERB MUSSELS

SERVES 4

1 tablespoon olive oil

2 cloves garlic, crushed

1 small red chili pepper such as serrano, seeded and finely chopped (optional)

2 large tomatoes, chopped

2 lb (1 kg) mussels, scrubbed and debearded

½ cup (4 fl oz/125 ml) dry red wine

1–2 tablespoons red wine vinegar

½ teaspoon salt

¼ cup (⅓ oz/10 g) chopped fresh flat-leaf (Italian) parsley

¼ cup (⅓ oz/10 g) chopped fresh basil

3 scallions (green onions), chopped

Place oil in rice cooker bowl, press "cook" and heat for 1 minute. Add garlic and chili (if using) and cook, stirring frequently, until aromatic, about 2 minutes. Add tomatoes and cook for 2 minutes. Add mussels (discarding any that do not close to the touch), wine, vinegar and salt. Close lid and cook, stirring occasionally, for about 8 minutes until mussels open. Discard any mussels that do not open. Stir in parsley, basil and scallions, reserving some for garnish.

Tip Cook ¾ lb (375 g) angel hair pasta in lightly salted water. Drain and toss with 1–2 tablespoons extra-virgin olive oil. Serve mussels on pasta, or toss mussels with pasta.

GARLIC AND CHILI SHRIMP

3 tablespoons olive oil
2 lb (1 kg) uncooked medium shrimp (prawns), peeled
and deveined, tails intact
2 small red chili peppers such as serrano or Thai,
seeded and thinly sliced
4 cloves garlic, thinly sliced
1/3 cup (1/2 oz/15 g) chopped fresh flat-leaf (Italian)
parsley or cilantro (coriander)

Place oil in rice cooker bowl, press "cook" and heat for 2–3 minutes. Add shrimp, chilis and garlic. Close lid and cook, stirring twice, until shrimp turn bright pink, 4–5 minutes. Garnish with parsley.

Tip Serve hot or cold with mixed green salad and crusty bread or toss with cooked pasta or rice.

TERIYAKI SHRIMP AND ASPARAGUS

SERVES 4

1/4 cup (2 fl oz/60 ml) teriyaki sauce
1/4 cup (2 fl oz/60 ml) sweet chili sauce
2 lb (1 kg) medium shrimp (prawns), peeled and
deveined, tails intact
2 tablespoons canola oil
2 bunches asparagus, 6–7 oz (180–220 g) each, ends
trimmed and spears cut on diagonal into 1-inch
(2-cm) pieces
1 lb (500 g) fresh hokkien or udon noodles, rinsed in
hot water
1/3 cup (1/2 oz/15 g) chopped fresh garlic chives

In a glass or ceramic bowl, stir together teriyaki and chili sauces. Add shrimp, stir to coat, cover and marinate for 15 minutes. Place oil in rice cooker bowl, press "cook" and heat for 2–3 minutes. Drain shrimp, reserving marinade. Add shrimp and asparagus to rice cooker bowl. Close lid and cook, stirring twice, until shrimp start to turn bright pink, 3–4 minutes. Add reserved marinade to noodles and cook until heated through, 2–3 minutes. Garnish with chives.

NGER-SCALLOP DUMPLINGS

SERVES 4

2 teaspoons peeled and grated fresh ginger
1 tablespoon Japanese soy sauce
1 tablespoon Chinese rice wine or sake
1 teaspoon Asian sesame oil
16 sea scallops
16 round wonton wrappers (gow gee)
2 scallions (green onions), finely chopped
3 oz (90 g) snowpeas (mange-tout), finely chopped
8 cups (64 fl oz/2 L) water
sweet chili sauce or plum sauce for serving

In a glass or ceramic bowl, stir together ginger, soy sauce, wine and oil. Add scallops, turn to coat, cover and marinate for 15 minutes. Place wonton wrappers on work surface and cover with a damp kitchen towel. Working with 1 wrapper at a time, place 1 scallop and some scallions and snowpeas in center of wrapper. Lightly brush edge of half of wrapper with water. Fold brushed side on dry side. Beginning at one end, gently press edges to seal and force out any excess air (excess air can cause wrapper to burst open during cooking). Set aside and cover with a damp kitchen towel. Repeat with remaining wrappers.

Put water in rice cooker bowl, close lid and press "cook." When water comes to a boil, add dumplings. Gently stir to prevent them from sticking together. Close lid and cook until dumplings float to surface and wonton wrappers are soft and translucent, 3–4 minutes. Remove with a slotted spoon. Serve with a drizzle of plum or sweet chili sauce.

Tip To steam dumplings, put water in rice cooker, close lid and press "cook." Line a steamer tray with parchment (baking) paper and arrange dumplings on prepared tray (leaving space around edges for steam to circulate). When water comes to a boil, put tray over water. Close lid and cook until wonton wrappers are soft and translucent, 5–6 minutes.

Tip To make ginger-scallop soup, cook dumplings in fish or chicken stock. Serve soup and dumplings garnished with scallions. Offer sauces on side.

MANGO, LIME AND GINGER FISH PARCELS

SERVES 4

¼ cup (2 fl oz/60 ml) Japanese soy sauce

2 tablespoons lime or lemon juice

1 tablespoon grated lime or lemon zest

4 scallions (green onions), chopped

1 tablespoon peeled and freshly grated fresh ginger

1 clove garlic, crushed

1 red chili pepper such as Thai or serrano, seeded and finely chopped (optional)

4 kaffir lime leaves, center rib removed and finely sliced

4 fish fillets or steaks, such as salmon, about 6 oz (180 g) each

2 mangoes, peeled, pitted, and sliced

1 cup (8 fl oz/250 ml) water

spiced Brown Rice (page 22)

In a bowl, stir together soy sauce, lime juice and zest, scallions, ginger, garlic, chili (if using) and lime leaves. Cut four 12-inch (30-cm) squares of parchment (baking) paper. Place a fillet or steak in center of each square. Place lime mixture and mango on top of fish, dividing evenly. Bring 2 opposite sides of paper over fish and fold twice to seal. Twist ends of parcel to close securely. Wrap each parcel in a 12-inch square of aluminum foil. Pour water into rice cooker bowl. Place fish parcels in cooker, arranging 2 on bottom and 2 across top. Close lid, press "cook" and cook for 3–4 minutes. Rotate parcels and cook until flesh flakes when tested with a fork, about 3–4 minutes longer. Timing will depend on thickness of fillets. Serve with brown rice.

Tips

- Place parcels on a steamer tray (or on a plate on top of a trivet) over water, press "cook," close lid and cook for 8–10 minutes, depending on thickness of fish.

- Substitute kaffir lime leaves with lemon grass. Slice or bruise the white section of lemongrass by gently hitting with a meat mallet or handle of knife.

- Substitute mango with peach.

SCRAMBLED EGGS WITH SMOKED SALMON AND LEMON CRÈME

SERVES 2

2 tablespoons crème fraîche or thick plain yogurt

2 teaspoons lemon juice

1 teaspoon unsalted butter

1 teaspoon olive oil

2 scallions (green onions), finely sliced

¼ cup (1½ oz/45 g) finely diced red bell pepper
(capsicum)

1 cup (2 oz/60 g) shredded spinach

4 large eggs, lightly beaten

¼ cups (2 fl oz/60 ml) milk or half milk and heavy
(double) cream

2 tablespoons chopped flat-leaf (Italian) parsley or
chives, optional

salt and cracked pepper

4 slices smoked salmon, cut into strips ¾ inch (2 cm)
wide

2 sprigs fresh dill for garnish

2 slices whole-grain bread, toasted

In a bowl, stir together crème fraîche and lemon juice; set lemon crème aside. Place butter and oil in rice cooker bowl, press "cook" and heat for 1 minute. When butter is melted, add scallions, bell pepper and spinach and cook, stirring occasionally, until spinach is wilted, about 2 minutes. In a bowl, stir together eggs, milk, and parsley if using, and season with salt and pepper. Pour into rice cooker bowl and gently stir until just cooked, 3–4 minutes. Serve topped with smoked salmon, lemon crème and dill. Accompany with toasted bread.

Tip Other ingredients, such as diced ham, diced tomato, diced celery, fresh corn kernels and/or pesto, can used to flavor eggs.

Vegetables

POTATO GRATIN

SERVES 4-6

1 tablespoon olive oil

1 yellow (brown) onion, sliced

1 lb (500 g) potatoes such as Desiree or Yukon gold

1 large sweet potato (kumera), about ¾ lb (375 g),
    peeled and thinly sliced

¾ cup (3 oz/90 g) grated Gruyère or Parmesan cheese

1½ cups (12 fl oz/375 ml) vegetable or chicken stock
    or water

½ cup (4 fl oz/125 ml) heavy (double) cream

Place oil in rice cooker bowl, press "cook" and heat for 1 minute. Add onion and cook, stirring occasionally, until onion softens slightly, about 2 minutes. Remove onion. Layer one-third potatoes, sweet potatoes and onion in bottom of rice cooker bowl. Sprinkle with one-third cheese, reserving 1 tablespoon for top. Continue making layers, finishing with sprinkling of cheese. Pour stock over vegetables. Close lid, press "cook" and cook until potatoes are soft when a knife is inserted in center of gratin, 35–40 minutes. Pour cream over vegetables. Close lid, press "cook" and cook for 5 minutes. Turn to "warm" and let stand for 10 minutes. If desired, invert heatproof plate over rice cooker bowl and invert plate and bowl together to unmold gratin. Place under a preheated broiler (grill) and broil (grill) until top is golden.

Tip Substitute pumpkin for some of the potato if desired.

THAI EGGPLANT, SQUASH AND LENTIL CURRY

SERVES 4

1 tablespoon peanut oil

1 large yellow (brown) onion, cut into wedges

1 clove garlic, crushed

¼ cup (2 fl oz/60 ml) Massaman curry paste

¾ lb (375 g) round Thai eggplants (aubergines), tops removed and quartered, or long Asian eggplants, diced

1 lb (500 g) butternut or other winter squash (pumpkin), peeled and cut into 1-inch (2.5-cm) cubes

1 cup (7 oz/220 g) dried red lentils, rinsed

3 cups (24 fl oz/750 ml) vegetable stock, or more if needed

2 teaspoons fish sauce

2 teaspoons sugar (optional)

1 cup (5 oz/155 g) fresh or frozen peas or green beans

2 kaffir lime leaves, center rib removed and finely sliced

2 tablespoons chopped fresh cilantro (coriander), optional

Add oil to rice cooker bowl, press "cook" and heat for 1 minute. Add onion and garlic and cook, stirring occasionally, until onion softens slightly, 2 minutes. Stir in curry paste and cook for 2 minutes. Add eggplants, squash, lentils, stock, fish sauce and sugar (if using). Close lid, press "cook" and cook until squash is tender when knife is inserted, about 20 minutes. Stir in peas and cook for 5 minutes, adding more stock if needed. Garnish with lime leaves and cilantro if using and serve with rice.

Tips Sauté diced firm tofu and cook with curry. Or place peeled and deveined shrimp (prawns) in steamer basket over curry and cook until bright pink, about 5 minutes. Serve shrimp on top of curry or carefully fold into curry. Stir 1 cup (8 fl oz/250 ml) coconut cream into curry for a creamier texture and flavor.

ASPARAGUS WITH BALSAMIC VINEGAR AND PARMESAN

SERVES 4

2 tablespoons olive oil
1 tablespoon balsamic vinegar
pinch salt
2 cups (16 fl oz/500 ml) water
2 bunches asparagus, 6–7 oz (180–220 g) each, ends trimmed
1/3 cup (1 1/2 oz/45 g) grated Parmesan cheese
cracked pepper

In a small bowl, whisk together oil, vinegar and salt; set aside. Put water in rice cooker bowl. Close lid and press "cook." When water comes to a boil, add asparagus. Close lid and cook until tender, 2–4 minutes, depending on thickness. Drain, transfer to a warmed bowl and drizzle with vinegar mixture. Sprinkle with Parmesan and season with pepper.

Tip Asparagus can also be cooked in a steamer tray placed over simmering water in rice cooker bowl for 3–5 minutes, depending on thickness.

BABY POTATOES WITH LEMON PEPPER

SERVES 4

16 small new potatoes, about 3 lb (1.5 kg) total
6 cups (48 fl oz/1.5 L) water or vegetable or chicken stock
1–2 tablespoons unsalted butter
1 teaspoon cracked pepper
1/2–1 teaspoon grated lemon zest

Put potatoes and water in rice cooker bowl. Close lid, press "cook" and cook until tender, about 10 minutes. Remove potatoes and discard water. Return rice bowl to cooker and add potatoes, butter, pepper and lemon zest, turning potatoes to coat with butter and seasonings. If desired, let stand on "warm" until serving.

Tip If cooking potatoes in stock, reserve stock and use for soups or sauces.

SPICY CORN ON THE COB

SERVES 4

2 tablespoons sweet chili sauce
2 tablespoons finely chopped fresh cilantro
  (coriander) or flat-leaf (Italian) parsley
1 teaspoon Asian sesame oil
pinch salt
4 ears of corn, husks removed
2 cups (16 fl oz/500 ml) hot water

In a small bowl, stir together chili sauce, cilantro, sesame oil and salt. Put corn in a shallow dish and drizzle with chili sauce mixture, turning to coat well. Cut four 12-inch (30-cm) squares of parchment (baking) paper or aluminum foil. Place 1 ear in center of each square. Bring 2 opposite sides of paper over corn and fold twice to seal. Twist ends of parcel to close securely. Place on a steamer tray. Pour boiling water into rice cooker bowl. Press "cook" and bring to a boil. Place steamer over water, close lid and cook until corn is tender, about 10 minutes.

Tip To cook parcels without using steamer tray, wrap each parcel in a 12-inch (30-cm) square of aluminum foil. Pour water in rice cooker bowl and set parcels in water. Cooking time will be slightly shorter.

CARAMELIZED SWEET POTATO WITH SESAME SEEDS

SERVES 4

4 cups (32 fl oz/1 L) water
1½ lb (750 g) sweet potatoes (kumeras), peeled and
  cut into 1 1/2-inch (4-cm) pieces
pinch salt
¼ cup (2 fl oz/60 ml) pure maple syrup
½ teaspoon ground cinnamon
2 teaspoons sesame seeds, toasted in a dry frying pan
  until golden

Put water, sweet potatoes and salt in rice cooker bowl. Close lid, press "cook" and cook until just tender, about 10 minutes. Remove potatoes with slotted spoon. Discard water. Return bowl to cooker and add potatoes, maple syrup and cinnamon. Press "cook," close lid and cook, turning once, until caramelized, 5–10 minutes. Serve sprinkled with sesame seeds.

Desserts

SPICED BLUEBERRY RICE

SERVES 4

1½ cups (½ oz/315 g) short- or medium-grain white
  rice, rinsed
1 cup (8 fl oz/250 ml) water
1 cup (8 fl oz/250 ml) apple or black currant juice
½ teaspoon ground cinnamon
¼ teaspoon salt
1 cup (4 oz/125 g) blueberries or strawberries
1 tablespoon lime or lemon juice
1 teaspoon grated lime or lemon zest
½ cup (2 oz/60 g) berry yogurt
⅓ cup (2 oz/60 g) hazelnuts (filberts), toasted
  (page 60) and coarsely chopped

Put rice, water, juice, cinnamon and salt in rice cooker bowl and stir to combine. Close lid and press "cook." Cook, stirring once, until rice cooker turns to "warm," about 15 minutes. Stir rice with a rice paddle, then fold in blueberries, juice and zest and yogurt. Close lid and let stand for 10 minutes on "warm." Sprinkle with hazelnuts.

Tip To make Blueberry Rice Brûlé, divide blueberry rice among ramekins and refrigerate. Sprinkle a thin layer of brown or Demerara sugar over rice in each ramekin. Place ramekins in preheated broiler (grill) until sugar turns golden, 3–4 minutes, being careful that sugar does not burn.

BLACK RICE WITH CHERIMOYA AND COCONUT CREAM

SERVES 4

1½ cups (10½ oz/315 g) Thai black rice, rinsed
2½ cups (20 fl oz/625 ml) water
½ teaspoon salt
¼ cup palm or brown sugar
1 cherimoya (custard apple) or mango
½ cup (2 fl oz/60 ml) coconut cream
2 teaspoons white sesame seeds, toasted in a dry
   frying pan until golden

Put rice in a bowl with water to cover and let stand overnight. Drain and put rice, water and salt in rice cooker bowl, spreading rice evenly in bottom of bowl. Close lid and press "cook." Cook until rice cooker turns to "warm," about 40 minutes. If using cherimoya, cut in half and scoop out flesh. Discard seeds. If using mango, cut flesh away from each side of pit. Peel each half and chop flesh. Stir chopped fruit and sugar into cooked rice. Close lid and let stand until heated through, 5–10 minutes. Swirl coconut cream through cooked rice and garnish with sesame seeds.

Tip Rice can also be served chilled.

CRANBERRY AND ORANGE RICE WITH PECANS

SERVES 4

1½ cups (12 fl oz/375 ml) water
1¼ cups (8½ oz/265 g) long-grain white rice, rinsed
1 cup (4 oz/125 g) fresh or dried cranberries
1 cup (8 fl oz/250 ml) orange juice
grated zest of 1 orange
¼ teaspoon cinnamon
¼ teaspoon salt
1 cup (2 oz/125 g) pecans, toasted and coarsely
   chopped

Combine water, rice, cranberries, orange juice and zest, cinnamon and salt in rice cooker bowl, spreading rice evenly in bottom of bowl. Close lid and press "cook." Cook, stirring occasionally, until rice cooker turns to "warm," 12–15 minutes. Serve garnished with pecans.

Tip After juicing oranges, reserve orange skins. Remove any orange flesh and spoon cranberry rice into skins to serve.

GINGER NUT AND FRUIT FLAN

SERVES 6–8

FOR CRUST

12 ginger cookies, about 6 oz (180 g) total

½ cup (2 oz/60 g) walnuts

1 teaspoon ground cinnamon or nutmeg

5 tablespoons (2½ oz/75 g) unsalted butter, melted

FOR FILLING

1 lb (500 g) rhubarb, cut into ¾-inch (2-cm) pieces

2 pears such as Bartlett or Comice, quartered
    lengthwise, cores removed and cut into slices
    ¼ inch (6 mm) wide

¾ cup (6 oz/180 g) sugar

¾ cup (6 fl oz/180 ml) water

1 tablespoon lime or lemon juice

2 teaspoons grated lime or lemon zest

1 teaspoon Japanese soy sauce

3 tablespoons cornstarch (cornflour) dissolved
    in ¼ cup (2 fl oz/60 ml) water

1 cup (4 oz/125 g) fresh or frozen blueberries or other
    berries

To make crust, place cookies in plastic bag and, using a meat mallet or rolling pin, crush until cookies are fine crumbs. (Using a food processor may strain motor.) Place walnuts in another plastic bag and crush. In a bowl, combine cookie crumbs, crushed walnuts and cinnamon. Stir in melted butter. Remove sides from an 8-inch (20-cm) springform pan. Place a sheet of parchment (baking) paper over pan bottom and replace sides. Do not trim sheet but allow to protrude from pan. Place crust mixture in pan and, using a flat-bottomed glass, press until evenly spread and firm. Refrigerate until needed.

To make filling, put rhubarb, pears, sugar, water, juice and zest and soy sauce in rice cooker bowl. Close lid, press "cook" and cook, stirring twice, until rhubarb starts to soften, 5–6 minutes. Gently stir cornstarch mixture and blueberries into rhubarb. Cook uncovered, stirring, until fruit thickens. Remove bowl from rice cooker and let filling cool but not set. Pour into crust. Refrigerate until set and chilled, 30 minutes.

Tip If rhubarb is very juicy, add 2 tablespoons extra cornflour to help mixture stiffen and set.

PEACHES IN PORT WITH HONEY YOGURT

SERVES 4

½ cup (1½ oz/45 g) flaked coconut
½ cup (2 oz/60 g) pecans, coarsely chopped
2–3 teaspoons unsalted butter
4 large peaches, 2 lb (1 kg) total, halved and pitted
½ cup (4 fl oz/125 ml) tawny port
½ cup (4 oz/125 g) thick plain yogurt
1 tablespoon honey
¼ teaspoon ground allspice or cinnamon

Put coconut and pecans in rice cooker bowl. Press "cook" and cook, stirring constantly, until coconut is golden, 3–4 minutes. Transfer to a plate. Wipe bowl with paper towels and return to cooker. Put butter in rice cooker bowl and press "cook." When butter is melted, working in batches, add peach halves, cut side down, and cook until golden, 2–3 minutes. Using plastic tongs, carefully remove peaches. Add port to rice cooker bowl and stir to release any cooked bits from bottom of bowl. Put peaches in rice cooker bowl, cut side up. Close lid and cook, turning once, until peaches are just beginning to soften, 6–8 minutes. Remove peaches. Press "cook" and cook liquid, uncovered, until thickened, about 2 minutes. In a bowl, stir together yogurt and honey. Put 2 peach halves on each plate. Top with honey yogurt and garnish with coconut and pecans. Drizzle sauce around peaches.

Tip Other fruits, such as nectarines, apricots and mango may be used in place of the peaches. Substitute toasted hazelnuts (filberts) (see page 60) or macadamias for pecans, and stir nuts and coconut into yogurt just before serving.

INDEX

WEIGHTS AND MEASUREMENTS

The conversions given in the recipes in this book are approximate. Whichever system you use, remember to follow it consistently throughout a recipe, to ensure proportions are correct.

Weights

Imperial	Metric
1/3 oz	10 g
1/2 oz	15 g
3/4 oz	20 g
1 oz	30 g
2 oz	60 g
3 oz	90 g
4 oz (1/4 lb)	125 g
5 oz (1/3 lb)	150 g
6 oz	180 g
7 oz	220 g
8 oz (1/2 lb)	250 g
9 oz	280 g
10 oz	300 g
11 oz	330 g
12 oz (3/4 lb)	375 g
16 oz (1 lb)	500 g
2 lb	1 kg
3 lb	1.5 kg
4 lb	2 kg

Volume

Imperial	Metric	Cup
1 fl oz	30 ml	
2 fl oz	60 ml	1/4
3 fl oz	90 ml	1/3
4 fl oz	125 ml	1/2
5 fl oz	150 ml	2/3
6 fl oz	180 ml	3/4
8 fl oz	250 ml	1
10 fl oz	300 ml	1 1/4
12 fl oz	375 ml	1 1/2
13 fl oz	400 ml	1 2/3
14 fl oz	440 ml	1 3/4
16 fl oz	500 ml	2
24 fl oz	750 ml	3
32 fl oz	1 L	4

Oven temperature guide

The Celsius (°C) and Fahrenheit (°F) temperatures in this chart apply to most electric ovens. Decrease by 25°F or 10°C for a gas oven or refer to the manufacturer's temperature guide. For temperatures below 325°F (160°C), do not decrease the given temperature.

Oven description	°C	°F	Gas Mark
Cool	110	225	1/4
	130	250	1/2
Very slow	140	275	1
	150	300	2
Slow	170	325	3
Moderate	180	350	4
	190	375	5
Moderately hot	200	400	6
Fairly hot	220	425	7
Hot	230	450	8
Very hot	240	475	9
Extremely hot	250	500	10

Useful conversions

1/4 teaspoon	1.25 ml
1/2 teaspoon	2.5 ml
1 teaspoon	5 ml
1 Australian tablespoon	20 ml (4 teaspoons)
1 UK/US tablespoon	15 ml (3 teaspoons)

Butter/Shortening

1 tablespoon	1/2 oz	15 g
1 1/2 tablespoons	3/4 oz	20 g
2 tablespoons	1 oz	30 g
3 tablespoons	1 1/2 oz	45 g

A LANSDOWNE BOOK

Published by Apple Press in 2005
Sheridan House
4th Floor
112-116 Western Road
Hove
East Sussex BN3 1DD UK

www.apple-press.com

Created and produced by Lansdowne Publishing
Text: Brigid Treloar
Photographer: Andre Martin
Stylist: Sarah O'Brien
Designer: Avril Makula
Editor: Judith Dunham
Production: Sally Stokes and Eleanor Cant
Project Coordinator: Kate Merrifield

ISBN 1-84543-063-8

Set in Meta Plus and Bembo on QuarkXPress
Printed in Singapore by Tien Wah Press (Pte) Ltd